31478000214784

P9-DFY-164

LIGHTNING BOLT BOOKS™

Can You Tell a Frog from a Toad?

Buffy Silverman

Lerner Publications Company

Minneapolis

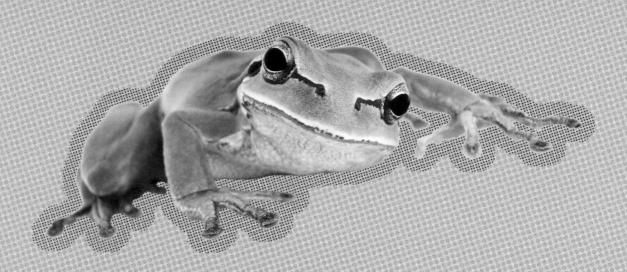

Copyright © 2012 by Lerner Publishing Group, Inc.

All rights reserved. International copyright secured. No part of this book may be reproduced, stored in a retrieval system, or transmitted in any form or by any means—electronic, mechanical, photocopying, recording, or otherwise—without the prior written permission of Lerner Publishing Group, Inc., except for the inclusion of brief quotations in an acknowledged review.

Lerner Publications Company
A division of Lerner Publishing Group, Inc.
241 First Avenue North
Minneapolis, MN 55401 U.S.A.

Website address: www.lernerbooks.com

Library of Congress Cataloging-in-Publication Data

Silverman, Buffy.
   Can you tell a frog from a toad? / by Buffy Silverman.
      p.   cm. — (Lightning bolt books.™—Animal look-alikes)
   Includes index.
   ISBN 978–0–7613–6732–1 (lib. bdg. : alk. paper)
   1. Frogs—Juvenile literature. 2. Toads—Juvenile literature. I. Title.
   QL668.E2S546 2012
   597.8'9—dc22   2011000688

Manufactured in the United States of America
2 – CG – 12/31/11

Contents

Rough or Smooth

Frogs and toads look a lot alike. As adults, they have no tail. They hop or leap on land.

Can you tell which of these animals is a frog and which is a toad?

Big eyes bulge from their heads. They shoot their sticky tongues out to catch insects.

This insect just became a meal! Frogs and toads also gulp spiders, worms, and other small animals.

But you can tell them apart. Most frogs have smooth skin. The skin makes a thick liquid called mucus. Mucus helps to keep skin moist.

Look at this toad's bumpy skin. A toad's skin is rougher and drier than a frog's skin. The bumps are called warts.

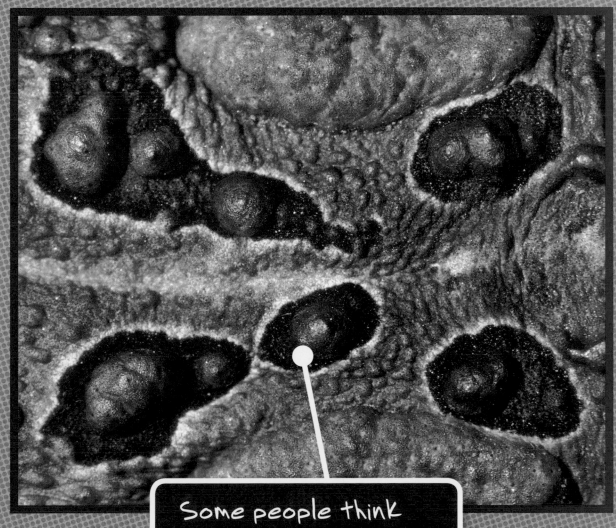

Some people think you can get warts from touching a toad. But this isn't true.

Frogs and toads breathe with lungs. But they also breathe through their skin. Their skin must stay moist for them to breathe.

Even a toad's dry skin has some moisture in it.

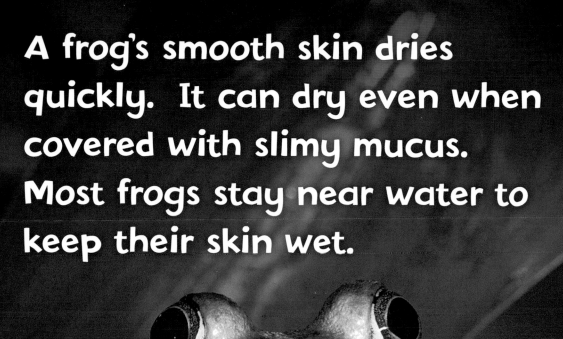

A frog's smooth skin dries quickly. It can dry even when covered with slimy mucus. Most frogs stay near water to keep their skin wet.

A toad's thick skin does not lose water as fast. Thick skin lets a toad live away from water. You might see a toad hopping around your backyard.

Leap or Hop

A leopard frog sits on the bank of a pond. A hungry raccoon steps near. The frog leaps into the water. It swims to the muddy bottom. Its long hind legs help it escape. Frogs jump and swim with long legs.

A toad makes short hops on short legs. It hops and walks across meadows, gardens, and forests.

A frog's body is often longer and thinner than a toad's body. Shorter, fatter toads do not jump as far as frogs.

A frog's legs are much longer than a toad's legs.

When frogs leap into water, their feet help them swim. Skin stretches between the toes of this frog's hind feet. **The skin is called webbing.** Webbed feet push water to help the frog move.

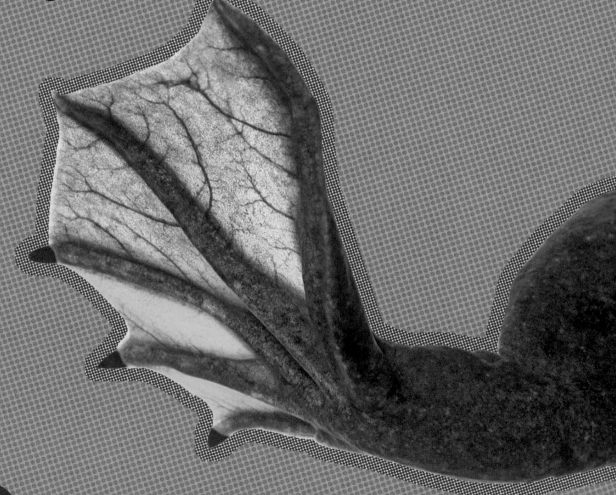

Toads that live on land have less webbing on their hind feet. They use their feet to walk and dig. When the weather is hot and dry, toads burrow into the ground. Some toads have special hard scoops on their hind feet.

This spadefoot toad's back feet help it dig.

Some frogs have less webbing too. A tree frog's feet are made for climbing. Round toe pads grip leaves and bark. Some tree frogs can climb up glass!

Staying Safe

A toad sits among dead leaves. Its dull-colored skin is hard to spot. Many toads stay safe by blending in with the ground. Blending in also helps them catch food.

Can you find the toad?

But some predators find toads. Predators are animals that hunt and eat other animals. Toads have two large glands on their backs. Poison oozes out of them. The poison burns. It keeps predators from eating the toad.

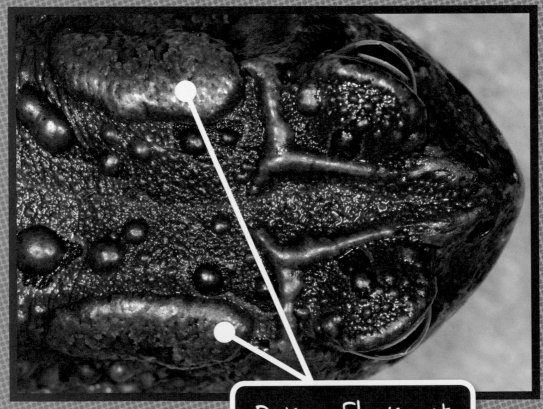

Poison flows out of these glands.

Many frogs also blend in with their homes. Bullfrogs hide among pond plants. If a predator strikes, the bullfrogs leap far or swim fast. Frogs have poison glands too. But most frogs' poison isn't strong enough to hurt a predator.

Most frogs' poison is weak. But this frog's poison is very dangerous.

Some frogs have bright colors. They don't blend in at all. These frogs are usually very poisonous. A poison dart frog hops along the forest floor. Its bright colors warn predators to stay away.

This toad has bright colors. But it hides them. Its green back blends with the ground. The toad flips over when a predator nears. Its black and red belly warns of poison.

Egg Time

Female frogs and toads both lay eggs in the springtime. They lay their eggs in puddles, ponds, and streams.

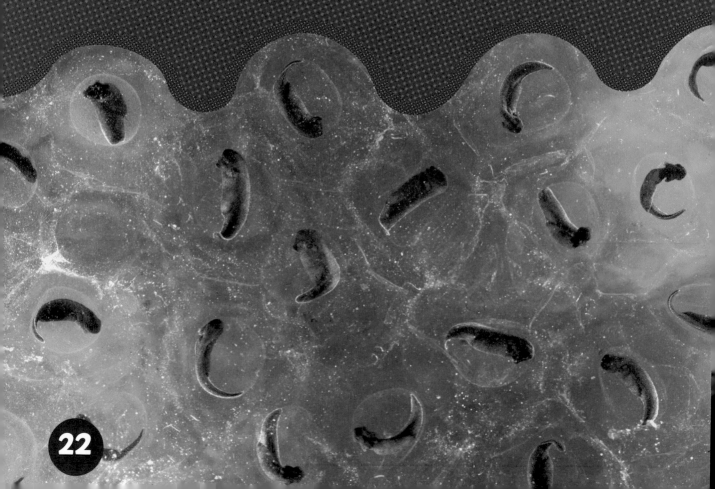

Frogs lay clumps of eggs. The eggs are covered in jelly. Other animals eat most of them.

Clear, thick jelly covers and protects these frog eggs.

Toads lay long chains of eggs. Predators eat most of these eggs too. But some survive.

A few frog or toad eggs hatch into tadpoles. Tadpoles live in shallow water. These baby frogs and toads breathe with gills. Tadpoles don't have legs.

Tadpoles breathe through gills like these.

They wriggle their tails and swim. They eat and grow. Slowly, tadpoles change into adults.

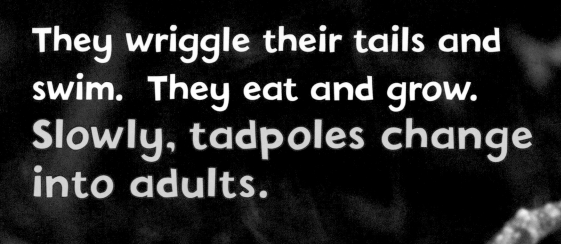

This tadpole is about twelve weeks old.

Watch for frogs and toads near ponds, lakes, and meadows.

Can you tell these look-alikes apart?

Who Am I?

Look at the pictures below. Which ones are frogs? Which ones are toads?

 Long legs let me leap into ponds.

Short legs let me hop on land.

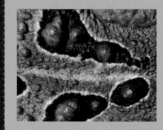 I have thick, rough skin.

I have smooth, moist skin.

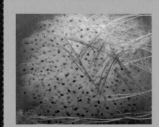 I lay eggs in clumps.

I lay long chains of eggs.

Answers:
column 1: frog, toad, frog; column 2: toad, frog, toad

Fun Facts

- More than four thousand different kinds of frogs live around the world. Scientists think of toads as part of the frog group.

- Many frogs can leap twenty times their body length. That is like you jumping the length of two school buses! The longest frog jump recorded is more than 33 feet (10 meters).

- When a snake grabs a toad, the toad blows its body up with air. That makes it hard for the snake to swallow. But snakes still eat many toads.

- Most frogs and toads do not take care of their eggs and tadpoles. But a few do. One type of frog that lives in Australia swallows her eggs. Tadpoles grow in her stomach. They hop out of her mouth as frogs.

Glossary

burrow: to dig a tunnel or hole in the ground for shelter

gill: a body part that some animals use for breathing underwater

gland: a body part that makes and releases chemicals

insect: an animal that has six legs and three main body parts as an adult

lung: a body part that some animals use for breathing air

mucus: a thick liquid that some animals make to keep their skin moist and protect it

predator: an animal that hunts and eats other animals

tadpole: a young frog or toad that has hatched from an egg

wart: a bump on a toad's skin

webbing: a thin layer of skin between an animal's toes

Further Reading

Bishop, Nic. *Frogs*. New York: Scholastic Nonfiction, 2008.

French, Vivian. *Growing Frogs*. Cambridge, MA: Candlewick, 2003.

Frog and Toad Calls
http://www.umesc.usgs.gov/terrestrial/amphibians/armi/frog_calls.html

National Geographic Animal Video: Bullfrogs Eat Everything
http://video.nationalgeographic.com/video/player/animals/amphibians-animals/frogs-and-toads/frog_bull.html

National Geographic Kids Creature Features: Red-Eyed Tree Frogs
http://kids.nationalgeographic.com/kids/animals/creaturefeature/red-eyed-tree-frogs

Ryder, Joanne. *Toad by the Road: A Year in the Life of These Amazing Amphibians*. New York: Henry Holt and Company, 2007.

Silverman, Buffy. *Do You Know about Amphibians?* Minneapolis: Lerner Publications Company, 2010.

Index

Photo Acknowledgments

The images in this book are used with the permission of: © Matt Antonino/Shutterstock Images, p. 1 (top); © jamie cross/Shutterstock Images, p. 1 (bottom); © Adam Gryko/Shutterstock Images, p. 2; © Joel Sartore/National Geographic/Getty Images, p. 4 (top); © Electrochris/Dreamstime.com, p. 4 (bottom); © Flirt/SuperStock, p. 5; © Chris Mattison/Alamy, pp. 6, 28 (center right); © Dwight Kuhn, pp. 7, 8, 9, 12, 17, 19, 22, 24, 25, 26, 28 (top right, center left, bottom right); © Janno Vään/Alamy, p. 10; © Oxford Scientific/Photolibrary, p. 11; © Michael Durham/Minden Pictures, pp. 13, 28 (top left); © Dorling Kindersley/Getty Images, p. 14; © O.S.F./Animals Animals, p. 15; © Gary Meszaros/Visuals Unlimited, Inc., p. 16; © David Kuhn, p. 18; © James P. Rowan, p. 20; © Eric Isselée/Shutterstock Images, p. 21; © Dr. Keith Wheeler/Photo Researchers, Inc., pp. 23, 28 (bottom left); © Jdeboer152/Dreamstime.com, p. 27 (top); © Jgade/Dreamstime.com, pp. 27 (bottom), 30; © FikMik/Shutterstock Images, p. 31.

Front cover: © Arco Images GmbH/Alamy (top); © Eric Isselée/Shutterstock Images (bottom).

Main body text set in Johann Light 30/36.